Antigone

BY SOPHOCLES

PRESTWICK HOUSE
LITERARY TOUCHSTONE CLASSICS™
P.O. BOX 658 • CLAYTON, DELAWARE 19938

SENIOR EDITOR: Paul Moliken

EDITOR: Elizabeth Osborne

TRANSLATOR: J.E. Thomas

COVER DESIGN: Kelly Valentine Vasami

PRODUCTION: Jerry Clark

PRESTWICK HOUSE
LITERARY TOUCHSTONE PRESS

P.O. BOX 658 • CLAYTON, DELAWARE 19938
TEL: 1.800.932.4593
FAX: 1.888.718.9333
WEB: www.prestwickhouse.com

ISBN 978-1-58049-388-8

Performance Note

Professionals and amateurs, please note that *Antigone* translated by J. E. Thomas is fully protected under the copyright laws of the United States and all countries within the copyright union. Performance rights are hereby granted for non-profit educational purpose. Performance rights for any for-profit purposes are reserved by the publisher. All inquirers related to obtaining performance rights and royalty rates for should be directed to Jerry Clark, Prestwick House, Inc. P.O. Box 658 Clayton, DE 19938.

CONTENTS

NOTES

What is a literary classic and why are these classic works important to the world?

A literary classic is a work of the highest excellence that has something important to say about life and/or the human condition and says it with great artistry. A classic, through its enduring presence, has withstood the test of time and is not bound by time, place, or customs. It speaks to us today as forcefully as it spoke to people one hundred or more years ago, and as forcefully as it will speak to people of future generations. For this reason, a classic is said to have universality.

Antigone has been read and performed for so many years because it raises questions that are pertinent in every age: How much power should the government have? What responsibility does a person have to act in accordance with his or her conscience? And can the answers to both of these questions coexist with one another?

Antigone also asks what we owe to our families. Complex relationships exist between Antigone and Ismene and between Creon and Haemon. Then, too, Antigone has a relationship with the dead brother she insists on burying; she feels that Ismene betrays this dead man.

Finally, it could be said that Antigone represents feeling, even intuition, while Ismene represents reason and caution. Seen in one light, Ismene is rational and Antigone is insane; on the other hand, Ismene is weak and Antigone is strong. Whether you support one sister or the other, you will find that this is a problem with no easy solution.

Reading Pointers for Sharper Insights

As you read *Antigone*, be aware of the following:

1. The conflict between civic responsibility and personal duty:

    *   Creon focuses exclusively on civic responsibility. He believes that a citizen's commitment to his city comes before all else; as ruler, his duty to the city is especially sacred. He says,

        > ...my country is
        > safety itself, and only when she is upright
        > can our sailing find friends. With laws like these
        > I will make our city grow.

        In the interest of Thebes, therefore, he declares that Eteocles will be buried, while Polynices will be left unburied:

    *   Antigone ignores civic responsibility and thinks only of the obligations to family sanctioned by traditional religion. She sees her duty to Polynices as a requirement of the gods. She breaks Creon's rule in the name of divine law, and even anticipates gaining the reputation of a "holy outlaw":

        > ...could my fame be more gloriously
        > established than by placing my brother
        > in a tomb?

2. The difficulty of resolving this conflict:

    *   Neither Creon nor Antigone is the hero of this play; both are inflexible, and both cause suffering by their stubbornness. Both, however, are noble characters driven by principle towards goals the Greek audience would recognize as morally good.

- Moreover, the character who advises compromise, Ismene, is no more heroic; in fact, she seems weak in comparison to her sister.

How does the conflict between two good characters with reasonable explanations for their actions make the plot more complicated than a play with a clear hero and villain?

SETTING

In front of the palace of Thebes, exactly as in Sophocles' *Oedipus Rex*. The sons of Oedipus, Eteocles and Polynices, originally agreed to share their father's kingship over Thebes, but soon afterwards Eteocles claimed sole power and drove Polynices into exile. Polynices found sanctuary and support in the powerful city of Argos, so much so that the king of Argos betrothed his daughter to Polynices. Raising an Argive army led by himself and six other famous heroes, Polynices marched on Thebes, where each of the city's seven gates was attacked by one of the heroes, who were slain there by a Theban hero, but Polynices and Eteocles fought and slew each other. On the morning our play opens, the Argive army has just left Theban territory; the city is filled with relief. Creon, brother to Oedipus' queen, has taken the kingship without controversy.

Dramatis Personae

ANTIGONE, *a young woman; daughter of Oedipus and Jocasta; betrothed to Haemon; niece of Creon; sister of Polynices, Eteocles, and Ismene*

ISMENE, *Antigone's sister*

CHORUS *of the old men of Thebes*

CREON, *king of Thebes; father of Haemon; uncle of Antigone & Ismene through his sister Jocasta, mother and wife of Oedipus*

GUARD *of the body of Polynices*

HAEMON, *son of Creon, betrothed to Antigone*

TIRESIAS, *blind prophet and priest of Apollo*

MESSENGER

EURYDICE, *wife of Creon*

2nd MESSENGER

ANTIGONE

Enter ANTIGONE *and* ISMENE *from the palace.*

ANTIGONE:
> Ismene, my dear sister through common blood,
> do you know of any evil from Oedipus
> Zeus[1] will not perform on us who still live? [2]
> For I have seen nothing—nothing painful,
> 5   nothing mad or shameful or dishonorable—
> that is not among your or my sorrows.
> And now what do they say? The general[3]
> has just put an edict over the whole city.
> Have you heard it? Or have you avoided
> 10   learning how our friends suffer the fate of foes?

ISMENE:
> No word of friends, Antigone, either
> sweet or painful, has come to me since we
> two sisters were robbed of our two brothers,
> both dying the same day by doubled hand.
> But since the army of the Argives
> 15   departed last night, I've seen nothing else,
> either to cause me to rejoice or to weep.

[1]*king of the gods, often portrayed as the supreme arbiter of justice and destiny*

[2]*See "Mythological Background" (page 65) for the story of Oedipus.*

[3]*Creon*

ANTIGONE:

> I knew it! For this reason I brought you
> outside the gates, that you alone might hear.

ISMENE:

> What? You seem to ponder something deeply.

ANTIGONE:

20   Indeed! For of our two brothers, Creon
> gives honorable burial to one,
> but dishonors the other. They say that
> he hid Eteocles beneath the earth
> with well-deserved pomp and circumstance,
25   as one honored among the dead below;
> but the corpse of Polynices, who died
> so sadly, they say it has been declared
> to the citizens that no one may bury
> or mourn him, but must see him unlamented,
30   unburied, a sweet find for birds to feast upon. [4]
> Such things they say our good Creon decreed
> for you and me—for me, I say!
> And he is coming here to announce it
> clearly to anyone who hasn't heard,
35   for he considers it no small matter,
> but for the one who does any of it,
> the penalty is death by public stoning.
> There you have it, and soon you will show
> how nobly you honor your noble birth.

ISMENE:

40   But what more, my poor girl, in times like these,
> could I do that would not tangle the knot further?

ANTIGONE:

> Will you share in the labor and the deed?

ISMENE:

> What is the venture? Where have your thoughts
>   gone?

[4] See "The Importance of Burial" (page 67) for information on Greek burial practices and the role played in them by women.

ANTIGONE:

Will you lift the corpse with this very hand? [5]

ISMENE:

45   You want to bury him, although it's forbidden in the city!

ANTIGONE:

I'll bury my brother—your brother, too,
though you refuse! I'll not be found a traitor.

ISMENE:

Madwoman, even when Creon forbids it?

ANTIGONE:

He has no right to keep me from my own.

ISMENE:

50   No, no! Think, my sister, how our father
died hated and infamous from offenses
self-detected, smiting both his eyes with
his very own hands. His wife and mother—
both words at once!—took her life with twisted noose;
55   then, third, our two brothers in just one day
slew each other, poor wretches, achieving
a common doom at one another's hands.
And now the two of us, left all alone—
think how very horribly we will die
60   if we go against the king's decree and strength
outside the law. Rather, consider that we
were born women, proving we should not fight with
          men,
and that we are ruled by more powerful people
and must obey them, even in more painful things.
65   Therefore I ask forgiveness from those below,
as I am forced to in these matters, and yield
to those who walk with authority.
For to do excessive things is nonsense.

ANTIGONE:

I would not order you; and if you change your mind

[5]*Greek has many words that indicate pointing. Antigone here would take Ismene's hand and indicate it.*

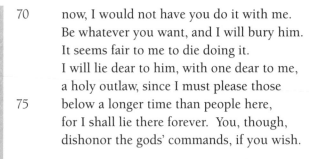

70   now, I would not have you do it with me.
      Be whatever you want, and I will bury him.
      It seems fair to me to die doing it.
      I will lie dear to him, with one dear to me,
      a holy outlaw, since I must please those
75   below a longer time than people here,
      for I shall lie there forever. You, though,
      dishonor the gods' commands, if you wish.

ISMENE:

      I do not dishonor them, but to do this
      against the state—I have no strength for it.

ANTIGONE:

80   Use that excuse, if you like, but I indeed
      will go and heap a tomb for my dearest brother.

ISMENE:

      Alas, how I fear for you, daring girl!

ANTIGONE:

      Don't worry for me; straighten out your own life.

ISMENE:

      Then, at least, proclaim this deed to no one;
85   but keep it secret, and I shall do the same.

ANTIGONE:

      Oh, denounce it! I will hate you the more
      if you don't tell these things to everyone.

ISMENE:

      You have a hot heart for chilling matters.

ANTIGONE:

      But I know I'll please those I should please most.

ISMENE:

90   If you can—you want the impossible.

ANTIGONE:

Well, then, I shall stop whenever my strength fails.

ISMENE:

You should not start an impossible quest.

ANTIGONE:

If you say this, you will be hateful to me,
and the dead will hate you always–justly.
95   But let me and my foolish plans suffer
this terrible thing, for I shall succumb
to nothing so awful as a shameful death.

ISMENE:

Then go, if this seems best to you, but know that
your friends truly love you, however foolish.

> Exit ANTIGONE *off stage,* ISMENE *into the*
> *palace, after which the* CHORUS *marches*
> *onto the stage.* 6

CHORUS:

6*See* parodos *in*
"*The Chorus*" *(page*
70)

                                            Str. 1

100   Ray of the sun,
fairest light of all those shining
on seven-gated Thebes,
at last you appeared,
O eyes of golden day,
105   coming over the streams of Dirce,7
you sent away the white-shielded warrior
from Argos, running from here,
with your piercing bridle.

7*one of the most*
famous landmarks
of Thebes

He set forth against our land
110   because of the contentious claims of Polynices,
like a sharply crying
eagle flying into our land,
covered with a wing white as snow,
descending with many shields
115   and crested with horse-hair.

Ant. 1

He perched on the roof,
gaping wide with bloody spears
around our seven gates,
but then he went away,

120 before his jaws were filled with our blood
or Hephaestus'[8] torches could take
our crown of towers.
Such a clash of Ares[9] swelled behind him,
a hard conquest for the dragon's rival. [10]

125 For Zeus hates excessively
the boasts of a great tongue, and looking on them
coming in rapid flow,
over-confident in clanging gold, he threw down
the one rushing with brandished fire

130 to the top of his goal,
seeking already to proclaim his victory.

Str. 2

He fell in an arc to the hard ground,
torch in hand, the one who with raging onslaught
furiously was breathing

135 with the rush of the most hateful winds.
But, those things went otherwise,
and great Ares sent them to
various fates, smiting them,
our chariot's strongest horse.[11]

140 Seven captains at our seven gates,
marshaled against equal foes, left
to Zeus the router bronze weapons,[12]
except those two wretches, who were
born of the same father and the same mother,

145 standing against each other with doubly slaying
          spears,
they both took an equal share of their common death.

Ant. 2

But since great-named Victory came,
rejoicing in answer with Thebes of many chariots,
let us enjoy oblivion

[8]*the god of fire, often used as a metonymy for fire itself*

[9]*the god of war, particularly its irrational aspect; often used to suggest war itself*

[10]*Legend said that Thebes was founded when Cadmus sowed a field with the teeth of a dragon, out of which sprang the citizens of Thebes.*

[11]*Chariot racing in the ancient world always placed the strongest, fastest horse on the right end. There were four horses to a chariot, who raced side-by-side.*

[12]*The victor in combat often dedicated the spoils of his victory, usually his opponent's armor, to a god in gratitude for the victory. Zeus the router would be a common choice for this dedication.*

150 of the recent wars
 and let us go to all the temples
 of the gods to dance through the
 night, and may Bacchus,[13] who
 has made Thebes shake, be our leader.
Enter CREON *from the palace.*
155 But here is the king of this land,
 Creon, son of Menoeceus, our new leader
 in this new situation given by the gods.
 What plan does he hold
 that he proposed this gathered
160 council of old men,
 summoning us by proclamation?

CREON:
 Gentlemen, the gods have set right again
 our city's affairs, after shaking them
 in a storm, and I have summoned you here
165 out of all the citizens, knowing well
 how you always revered the power of
 Laius' throne; then, both when Oedipus saved
 the city and when he fell, you stood in
 consistent support of their children.[14]
170 And so, since in the same day they both fell
 by twofold fate, each striking and spreading
 fratricidal pollution, now I hold
 sole power and the throne, because I am
 the closest relative of the fallen.
175 It is impossible to know the soul,
 the mind, and character of any man,
 until he has proven himself in the law.
 For if someone rules an entire city
 and does not take hold of the best counsels,
180 but holds his tongue out of fear, I think him
 to be the worst of men, now and always;
 and the man who considers more important
 than his fatherland his friend, I think him
 worthless. For—and may all-seeing Zeus
185 be my witness—I would never be silent
 if I saw madness creeping among

[13]*the god of wine and intoxication; son of Zeus and a mortal princess of Thebes, hence his close association with Thebes*

[14]*Laius was Oedipus' father. See "Mythological Background" (page 65) for more information. "Their children" refers to Eteocles and Polynices.*

the citizens in place of salvation,
nor would I consider an enemy
of my country a friend to myself,
190   recognizing this: that my country is
safety itself, and only when she is upright
can our sailing find friends. With laws like these
I will make our city grow. Therefore, I
have made a decree to the citizens
195   concerning the sons of Oedipus:
Eteocles, who fell fighting for this city,
who earned every prize of valor,
will be buried and receive all honors
that go to the best of the dead below.
200   His erstwhile kinsman, however, I mean
Polynices, who returned from exile
with hopes of burning his native land and
ancestral gods from top to bottom,
wishing to feast on kindred blood and lead
205   the rest into slavery, it has been
decreed that in this city he shall be
neither buried nor mourned by anyone,
but everyone must leave him unburied,
a feast for birds and dogs, an outrage to see.
210   This is my judgment, and never from me
will the base take equal honor to the good;
but whoever is friendly to this city will
in life and death be equally honored by me.

CHORUS:
    You are at your pleasure to decide this,
215   son of Menoeceus, concerning the city's
friend and foe. You may use any habit both
with the dead and with all of us who live.

CREON:
    Then I would have you keep watch over my words.

CHORUS:
    Give this task to a younger man to do.

CREON:

220   No, the corpse's guards are already posted.

CHORUS:

    What would you have us do beyond this?

CREON:

    Do not join with those disobeying it.

CHORUS:

    No man is so foolish as to lust for death.

CREON:

    And truly that is this deed's reward, but

225   often profit has destroyed men through their hopes.

Enter GUARD from offstage.

GUARD:

    My lord, I will not say that I come breathless
    from rushing or quickly moving my feet,
    for often my thoughts stopped me in my place,
    and I'd wheel around on the road back where I came.

230   My heart kept talking to me, telling me,
    "Poor fool, why are you going where you're sure
    to be punished?" "Idiot, you stopping
    again? If Creon hears it from someone else,
    then you'll really pay for it!" Twisting like this

235   I made my way, the opposite of haste,
    and thus a short road became a long one.
    But, at last, the vote for coming won the day.
    Even if I have nothing to say, I'll tell you
    anyway, for I came seized by one hope,

240   to suffer nothing but my fated doom.

CREON:

    Why is it you have this lack of spirit?

GUARD:

    I wish to tell you first my side of it,

for I neither did the deed nor saw him
who did, nor do I deserve any harm.

CREON:

245   You're really trying to talk around the problem.
Clearly you have something new to report.

GUARD:

Terrible things make a man hesitate.

CREON:

Then why don't you speak and go away free?

GUARD:

And I'm saying it! Just now someone has
250   buried the corpse and gone off, sprinkling dust
over its flesh and performing the due rites.[15]

15*Sprinkling dust over the body was the crucial step to bring the spirit peace.*

CREON:

What did you say? What man has dared to do this?

GUARD:

I don't know, for there was no stroke of a
mattock or heap from a shovel, just hard
255   earth and dry land, unbroken, no trace
of wheels, but the workman worked without sign.
When the day watch first showed it to us, we
all thought it a most distressing marvel.
For, although he was hidden from sight,
260   he wasn't entombed *per se*, but there was
a little dust on him, as from one fleeing
a curse.[16] Yet there weren't any signs of beasts
or a dog coming near him, nor did the body
seem mangled. Evil words broke out among us,
265   guard accusing guard, and it would have come
to blows in the end, for there was no one
to stop us. Every single man stood
on trial, but none could be convicted,
everyone claimed he knew nothing.
270   We were ready even for trial by ordeal,

16*Anyone passing an unburied corpse who did not throw some dust over it would come under a curse from the ghost of the corpse.*

to walk through fire, to swear to the gods
that we had neither done the deed nor been
privy to the planning or the doing.
At last, when our investigation came
275   to nothing, one man spoke up, who caused us
all to nod our heads to the ground in fear,
for we had no alternative to what
he said or a safe course for ourselves
if we obeyed. His idea was that
280   this deed must be brought to you and not concealed.
This idea prevailed, and the lot chose
unhappy me to take this good office.
So here I am, unwilling—I know well—
among the unwilling, for no one
285   cherishes the messenger of evil words.

CHORUS:
My lord, my mind has long been counseling
that perhaps this was the work of the gods.

CREON:
Stop, before you say something to really
anger me and show yourself both old and foolish!
290   You speak insufferably when you claim
the gods have some concern for this carcass.
Would they honor him as a benefactor
and bury him, who came to set fire to
their temples girt with columns, to scatter
295   their donations, earth, and laws? Or do you
revere gods who honor evil men?
It isn't so. Rather, even before,
men in the city resisted this decree
and mumbled against me secretly,
300   shaking their heads and refusing to bear
the yoke as they should, to gratify me.
These guards here have been bribed—I can see that
clearly—by such men to do this, for no
institution has so harmed humanity
305   as the creation of money. It's destroyed
even cities, it has expelled men from

their homes; it teaches the minds of honest
men to deviate and take up foul things.
It has shown men how to be villainous
310   and to know every sort of godlessness.
However many did this for money
have brought punishment upon themselves, but,
since Zeus truly has my reverence still,
know this well, and I will say an oath before you:
315   unless you find the culprit of this tomb
and bring him before these eyes of mine,
Death alone will not protect you:
you'll all be hanged alive to demonstrate
your insolent crime, so the rest of your lives
320   you may steal, knowing once and for all
what sort of reward it brings, and learn that
we must not love all profit equally.
For you should know that more men suffer
from shameful gains than are saved by them.

GUARD:
325   May I say something, or should I just turn and go?

CREON:
You have annoyed me just by saying that!

GUARD:
Does it sting in the ears or in your soul?

CREON:
Why do you care where my pain is located?

GUARD:
The doer troubles your mind, I your ears.

CREON:
330   Oh, it is clear you were born a babbler.

GUARD:
Regardless, I would never do the deed.

CREON:

> You have, and you have sold your soul for cash.

GUARD:

> Alas!
> It's terrible when the one who judges judges wrong.

CREON:

335
> Quibble now about judgments; but if you
> don't show me who did this, you will affirm
> that foul profits reap terrible rewards.

> *Exit* CREON *into the palace.*

GUARD:

> Well, I hope we do find him! But whether
> he's taken or not—for chance controls that—
340
> there's no way you'll see me coming back here.
> Even now beyond my hope and thought I've
> been saved and owe the gods some gratitude.

> *Exit* GUARD *offstage.*

CHORUS:[17]

Str. 1

> This world has many wonders,
> but nothing is more wondrous than humanity.
345
> It crosses even the grey sea
> with a stormy south wind,
> passing under churning waves in open water;
> and the oldest of the gods,
> immortal, inexhaustible Earth,
350
> it wears away.
> With ploughs it winds back and forth,
> year after year,
> turning up the soil with the offspring of horses.[18]

Ant. 1

> He captures and takes
355
> the blithe tribe of birds
> and the races of beasts
> and the salty brood of the sea
> in the coils of woven nets,

[17] *The first stasimon. See page 70.*

[18] *mules*

360   a very skillful man. He rules
with devices the mountain haunts
of the wild animal
and tames the shaggy-necked horse
with a yoke on its back
and the tireless mountain bull.

Str. 2

365   He taught himself language and wind-like
thought and city-ruling urges,
how to flee the slings of frost
under winter's clear sky
and the arrows of stormy rain, ever-resourceful.
370   Against no possibility
is he at a loss.
For death alone he finds no aid,
but he has devised escape
from impossible diseases.

Ant. 2

375   With clever creativity beyond expectation,
he moves now to evil, now to good.
The one who observes the laws of the land
and justice, our compact with the gods,
is honored in the city, but there is no city
380   for one who participates in what is wrong
for the sake of daring.
Let him not share my hearth,
nor let me share his ideas
who has done these things.

The GUARD *returns onstage, leading* ANTIGONE.

385   What strange omen now confuses
my sight? How can I deny that
I know this young girl is Antigone?
O poor child of your poor father, Oedipus,
what is this? Have they somehow caught you
390   breaking the king's laws, found you
doing something foolish?

GUARD:

Here she is who did the deed, she's the one
we found burying him—but where is Creon?

Enter CREON *from the palace.*

CHORUS:
Here he comes from the house, and just in time!

CREON:
395   What is it? What chance makes my coming timely?

GUARD:
My lord, a mortal should never swear that
something cannot happen, for hindsight makes
liars of our plans. Just now I swore I'd
never come back here, because of those threats
400   you shot at me, but the greatest pleasure
is the joy you didn't even hope for.
I came here, despite my oaths to the contrary,
bringing this girl, who was captured performing
the rites of burial. This time no lot
405   was shaken; no, this one was my good luck,
no other's. Now then, my lord, you take her,
as you wish, and question and sentence her.
I've justly freed myself from these troubles.

CREON:
But to bring her? Where did you find her? How?

GUARD:
410   She was burying the man; you know it all.

CREON:
Do you really mean what you're saying?

GUARD:
I saw her burying the very corpse you
forbade. Am I speaking clearly enough?

CREON:
And how was she seen and caught in the act?

GUARD:

415   This is how it happened: When we came back,
threatened by those terrible things you said,
we brushed off all the dust that was covering
the body, left the clammy thing well and
truly bare. Then, we lay under shelter
420   of the highest hills, fleeing the foul stench;
each man tossing reproaches back and forth,
if any man's attention strayed from this task,
It was that time when the bright circle of
the sun stands in the middle of the sky
425   and the heat burns; suddenly a cyclone
lifted up from the earth a storm of dirt,
a distress of heaven, it fills the plain,
tormenting and ripping apart the trees.
The whole sky was filled. We just closed our eyes
430   and rode out the divine storm. After a while,
it ended, the girl was seen, who was wailing
bitterly like the shrill voice of a bird
who sees her empty nest, stripped of its nurslings.
Thus she screamed, when she saw the uncovered
435   body: She groaned loudly and called down evil
curses on whoever had done the work.
Immediately she gathered dry dust
in her hands and from a jug of fine bronze
lifted up she crowned the corpse with three-fold
440   libations. We saw it and rushed forward,
caught her quickly, completely unperplexed.
We questioned her both about the previous
incident and the current; she stood in
denial of nothing, something for me
445   both sweet and painful, all at once. Nothing
is sweeter than escaping trouble for
yourself, but it's painful to conduct friends
into it. But, for me, everything
takes second place to my own safety.

CREON:

450   You there, staring down at the ground, speak up:
do you affirm or deny doing these things?

ANTIGONE:

I assert that I did it; I do not deny it.

CREON:

You, then, may take yourself where you will,

Exit GUARD.

rescued from a heavy charge. But, you,
455   tell me briefly, not at length: did you know
it had been announced not to do this?

ANTIGONE:

I did. Why would I not know? It was clear.

CREON:

And yet you dared to overstep these laws?

ANTIGONE:

Because it wasn't Zeus who pronounced these
460   things to me, nor did Justice, companion
of the gods below, establish such laws
for humanity. I would never think
your pronouncements had such strength that, being
mortal, they could override the unwritten,
465   ever-lasting prescriptions of the gods,
for those aren't something recently made, but
live forever, and no one knows when they
first appeared. I did not intend to pay
the penalty to the gods for violating
470   these laws in fear of some man's opinion,
for I know I will die. How could I not,
Even if you had not proclaimed it? But
if I die before my time, I say this
is an advantage. Anyone who lives
475   a life of sorrow as I do, how could
they not count it a blessing to die?
Therefore, there is no pain for me in meeting
this fate, whereas if I were to endure
that one born from my mother die unburied,
480   that would cause me pain. As it is, I feel
nothing. If, however, I seem to you

to have acted foolishly, then perhaps
I owe my foolishness to a fool.

CHORUS:

485   She's clearly the fierce daughter of a fierce
father; she doesn't know to bend with the wind.

CREON:

But know that hard minds fall the hardest, and
that iron, so powerful of itself,
baked to exceeding hardness, you might see
490   crack and break into pieces. I know that
spirited horses are broken with a small bit,
for no one is allowed to think big thoughts,
if he is another man's slave. She showed
herself capable of insolence then,
495   going beyond the laws put before her.
Her second insolence, after she had
done it, was to exult in her deed and
laugh that she had done it. Now I am no man,
but she is a man, if power lies with her
500   with impunity. No, even if she
were closer than my sister's child, closer
than any who share my family's chapel,
she and her sister will not escape the
worst fate, for that girl as well I charge as
505   equal in plotting this burial. Her, too,
bring her here, for I've just seen her inside
in fury, not like someone in full control
of her senses. The heart of one who weaves
wickedness in darkness is usually
510   convicted beforehand. I, for my part,
hate anyone caught in the act who tries
to beautify his crimes thereupon.

ANTIGONE:

Do you want something more than killing me?

CREON:

Nothing more; I have that, and I have it all.

ANTIGONE:

515   Then why wait? Nothing you say gives me the
slightest pleasure—I pray nothing you say
ever will—and by nature I offend you.
And yet, could my fame be more gloriously
established than by placing my brother
520   in a tomb? I think all these people would
agree, if fear did not hold their tongues.
Tyranny is lucky in many ways,
above all in doing and saying what it will.

CREON:

You alone of all Cadmus' race think this.

ANTIGONE:

525   These think it, too, but hold their tongues for you.

CREON:

Aren't you ashamed to think differently from them?

ANTIGONE:

There's no shame in revering one from the same womb.

CREON:

And no brother died for the other side?

ANTIGONE:

A brother by the same mother and father.

CREON:

530   Why then this honor insulting to him?

ANTIGONE:

The dead man would not agree with you.

CREON:

If you honor him equally with the wicked.

ANTIGONE:

This was not his slave who died, but his brother!

CREON:

> Ravaging this land, while he stood in her defense!

ANTIGONE:

[19] the name both for
the underworld and
its king

535   Nevertheless, Hades[19] requires these rites.

CREON:

> The good don't want to share honors with the bad.

ANTIGONE:

> Who knows what is considered righteous below?

CREON:

> An enemy is not a friend, even when dead.

ANTIGONE:

> I cannot share their hate, only their love.

CREON:

540   Then go below, and if you must be loved,
> love them! No woman will rule while I live.

Enter ISMENE *from the palace.*

CHORUS:

> But here is Ismene before the doors,
> tears running down her cheeks out of love for her
>   sister.
> A shadow over her flushed brow
545 disfigures her face,
> staining her lovely cheek.

CREON:

> You—like a creeping viper you hid in
> my house, poisoning me. I did not know
> I was nurturing two blights to rebel
550 against my throne. Come, tell me—will you also claim
> a share of this funeral? Do you deny it?

ISMENE:
> I did the deed, if she consents,
> and I will take and bear the charge.

ANTIGONE:
> But Justice will not allow this to you,
555 since neither did you want nor did I share it.

ISMENE:
> But, in your time of trouble, I am not
> ashamed to sail those stormy seas beside you.

ANTIGONE:
> Death and the dead will witness who did the deed;
> I love no friends who are only friends in words.

ISMENE:
560 No, sister, do not dishonor me, but let
> me die with you and honor him who died.

ANTIGONE:
> You may not die with me, nor call yours that
> which you did not touch. My death is enough.

ISMENE:
> Could I desire life when you have left me?

ANTIGONE:
565 Ask Creon, since you are his protector.

ISMENE:
> Why do you grieve me if it does not help yourself?

ANTIGONE:
> If I mock you, I do so with pain.

ISMENE:
> But now—what can I do to help you now?

ANTIGONE:
> Save yourself. I do not grudge you your escape.

ISMENE:
570   Poor girl, am I to have no share in your fate?

ANTIGONE:
> Because you choose to live, and I to die.

ISMENE:
> But not with my arguments left unspoken.

ANTIGONE:
> You seem clever to some, I to others.

ISMENE:
> Then the error is equal for us both.

ANTIGONE:
575   Cheer up. You live, but my soul has been dead
> a long time, that I might serve the dead.

CREON:
> I declare that both these children are fools,
> one just become so, one her whole life.

ISMENE:
> Indeed, my lord, what sense we had does not
580   stand by us in troubles, but goes away.

CREON:
> For you, at least, choosing bad deeds with bad people.

ISMENE:
> What would life be for me alone, without her?

CREON:
> Do not speak of her; she is already gone.

ISMENE:
You would kill the bride of your own son?

CREON:
585   There are other fields just as fertile.

ISMENE:
Not with such harmony as he has with her.

CREON:
I do not want bad wives for my sons.

ISMENE:
Dearest Haemon, how your father injures you!

CREON:
You annoy me...and this marriage of yours.

ISMENE:
590   Will you really rob your son of this girl?

CREON:
Death himself will stop this wedding for me.

ISMENE:
It is determined, it seems, that she shall die.

CREON:
For you and me both! Waste no more time, but
bring them inside now, maids. From now on, they
must be women and not wander free, for
595   even brave men flee, when they see Death so close.
        Exit ANTIGONE *and* ISMENE *with Servants into the house.*

CHORUS:[20]

Str. 1

Truly blessed are those who have not tasted evil,
for to them whose house is shaken by the gods,
no species of madness is left out, creeping over the
majority of the family—

[20]*the 2nd* stasimon

600 like the swell of the salt sea when
the sea's darkness runs upon angry Thracian winds,
it churns up murky sand
from the deep and the storm-swept
promontories, beaten by the opposing waves, roar
    with lamentation.

Ant. 1

605 I see that the old woes of the house of
the Labdacids add to the woes of the dead,
nor does the new generation deliver its race, but one
    of the gods throws them down.
They have no release, for now light has fallen on
the last root of the house of Oedipus.
610 Bloody ashes of the lower gods
now mow her down in turn,
along with the folly of argument and fury of wits.

Str. 2

O Zeus, what human transgression
could limit your power?
615 All-catching Sleep never takes it,
nor the unwearied months of the gods,
but as never-decaying master,
you hold the brilliant radiance of Olympus.
The law will prevail,
620 in time that is, time to come,
as in all time past.
Nothing comes assuredly
to every mortal life—nothing but the rush to ruin.

Ant. 2

For indeed wide-ranging hope
625 is a blessing to many men,
but to many also a trick of light-minded desires.
It comes to one who knows nothing
until he burns his foot
walking in hot fire.
630 Hence the old saying still shows its wisdom:
Sometimes the bad seems good
to one whose wits
God leads to madness.
He will last a short time without ruin.

635	But here is Haemon, the last and youngest
	of your children![21] Does he come
	in grief for the fate of his
	intended bride, the maiden Antigone,
	in mourning for the bed he was cheated out of?

CREON:

640	We will soon know better than predictions.
	Son, can it be that you have heard my final
	vote and come to fight your father for your bride?
	Or am I your friend whatever I do?

HAEMON:

	Father, I am yours, and as you have me,
645	you guide the best course for me to follow.
	No marriage will ever be more important to
	me than justly carrying out your precepts.

CREON:

	And that, child, is how you ought to keep your
	affections: Stand by your father's ideas
650	in all things. This is why a man prays to
	have obedient children in his house:
	that they may take vengeance on their father's
	enemy in bad times and honor his friends
	as he himself does. But, whoever sires
655	useless children—what could you say except
	he has created problems for himself
	and much laughter for his enemies?
	My boy, never give up your wits for a
	woman because of the pleasure, knowing
660	that this darling becomes cold in your arms,
	your wife a wicked concubine in your house.
	And what wound could be worse than a bad friend?
	Therefore, spit her out like an enemy
	and let her find a husband in Hell.
665	Since I caught her, alone of all entire
	people, in open rebellion, I will not
	make myself a liar to the city,
	but kill her. So, let her call on the Zeus

[21]*Creon's older son, Megareus, died to save Thebes from the Argive army. See "Mythological Background."*

22 *Zeus Herceius, to whom there was an altar where members of a family sacrificed and worshipped together.*

of kinship,22 for if I nurture defiance
670   in my relatives, I'd surely have to
for those outside my clan. Whoever is
a good man at home is shown to be just
in the city, too, but whoever goes
outside the laws or violates them, or
675   thinks to give commands to his superiors,
this man will not meet praise from me. Rather,
whomever the city chooses must be
obeyed in all things—small, just, and the opposite.
And this man, I would wager, rules fairly
680   and would want to be ruled well, and when marshaled
under a cloud of spears, he would stand,
a good and just fighter in the front ranks.
No evil is worse than disobedience.
This one thing destroys cities, turns homes upside
685   down, it leads to the rout of allied armies;
while those who live uprightly are saved by
obedience. Therefore, rulers must be
supported, and we must not yield to women.
It would be better, if it had to be,
690   to fall at a man's hands and not to be called
worse than a woman.

CHORUS:
To us, at least, if we are not deceived
by age, you seem to speak what you say wisely.

HAEMON:
Father, the gods endow human beings
695   with intelligence, which is the greatest
of all possessions. I could never—
I don't know how I could say you don't
speak correctly, but sometimes another
man's opinion is also right. You, however,
700   cannot watch everything that people
say or do or blame, for the common men
out of fear of your face won't say such words
as you would not rejoice to hear; but I
can hear these things in darkness, how the city

705   weeps for this girl, says she's the least worthy
       of all women to die so badly for
       such noble deeds. "She didn't let her brother,
       who had fallen in combat, lie unburied,
       to be devoured by some ravenous
710   dog or bird. They ought to give her an award!"
       So the report spreads in darkness. When you
       do well, father, I have no more honored
       possession than that, for what prize is greater
       for children than a father's fame when he's
715   prospering? Or a son's for his father?
       Don't be so stubborn that you say you and
       you alone are right. Whoever thinks that
       he's the only one who can think or use
       his tongue or soul, no one else—these men, when
720   you open them up, are seen to be hollow.
       But, for a man to learn, even a wise man,
       is nothing shameful, nor to learn to bend
       and give way. You see how, in the winter
       storms, the trees yield that save even their twigs,
725   but those who oppose it are destroyed root and branch.
       Just so the captain who never slackens
       his sail once he's stretched it gets his boat turned
       and sails the rest with benches upside down.
       Rather, yield your anger and let yourself change.
730   Even though I'm young, a good idea
       might come from me: It would be best by far
       that man be born full of all the knowledge
       there is, but, if it usually happens
       not to turn out that way, to learn from those
735   who speak well is a good substitute.

CHORUS:
       My lord, if someone speaks in season, you should learn,
       and you also, for both sides have spoken well.

CREON:
       At our age, taught reason by a man so young?

HAEMON:

    Taught nothing that is not just! If I am young,
740   I do not need more time to study what's right.

CREON:

    So, what's right includes revering anarchists?

HAEMON:

    I'd never tell someone to revere the wicked!

CREON:

    Then she has not been taken by this disease?

HAEMON:

    Her fellow-citizens in Thebes deny it.

CREON:

745   The city will tell me how I ought to rule it?

HAEMON:

    Do you hear how rash and young *you* sound?

CREON:

    Should I rule this land for myself or for others?

HAEMON:

    This city does not belong to one man!

CREON:

    Isn't the city thought to be her ruler's?

HAEMON:

750   You'd be a good monarch for a desert.

CREON:

    It seems he's an ally of the woman.

HAEMON:

    If you are a woman! I care only for you!

CREON:

> Worst of all men, at odds with your own father!

HAEMON:

> Not when I see you at odds with justice.

CREON:

755   Am I wrong to protect my own empire?

HAEMON:

> You don't protect it when you trample the
> honors of the gods!

CREON:

> Disgusting character!
> To play the second to a woman!

HAEMON:

760   I would rather yield to her than to evil.

CREON:

> In any case, this whole speech is for her.

HAEMON:

> And for you and me and the gods below!

CREON:

> You cannot marry her while alive.

HAEMON:

> Then she will die and, dying, destroy another.

CREON:

765   Do you dare to threaten me so boldly?

HAEMON:

> What threat is it to speak my resolve to you?

CREON:

> You will regret teaching what you do not know.

HAEMON:
> Were you not my father, I would call you a fool.

CREON:
> You're the slave of a woman, don't chatter at me.

HAEMON:
770　Will you make arguments, but hear no answer?

CREON:
> Really? Then know, by Olympus, that you
> shall not revile me with insults and rejoice!
> Bring the hated thing, so that she may die
> at once, close by the eyes of her bridegroom.

HAEMON:
775　No, not in my sight—never think this can
> happen! She'll not die beside me, and you will
> never lay your eyes upon my face again,
> so rage with any of your friends who can bear it.
>
> *Exit* HAEMON *offstage.*

CHORUS:
> My lord, the man has gone quick with anger;
780　his mind, at that age, bears pain violently.

CREON:
> Let him go and think superhuman thoughts,
> but he will not save these girls from their doom.

CHORUS:
> Do you intend to kill both of them?

CREON:
> You're right—not the one who didn't touch him.

CHORUS:
785　How do you intend to kill the other?

CREON:

I shall take her to a place completely
devoid of human life and hide her, living,
in a rocky cavern. I'll put in with her
as much food as will ward off a curse, so that
790   our city will escape all pollution.[23]
There she can pray to Hades, the only god
she worships, and perhaps she will find a way
not to die—or learn, though too late for her,
that it is excessive work to love the dead.

CHORUS:[24]

                                                Str. 1

795   Love, unconquered in battle,
Love, who attacks wealth,
who sleeps on a young girl's soft cheek
and wanders beyond the sea and in the wilderness:
There is no escape from you for immortals
800   or men who live but for a day;
he who has you is mad.

                                                Ant 1

You guide even just men's minds
towards injustice, to their destruction.
You have even shaken up this kin strife,
805   through her glances, clear desire of the bride
is victorious, Love the coadjutor
in the great laws of old, for
Aphrodite, the irresistible goddess, is laughing.

Enter ANTIGONE *from the palace, led by* GUARDS.

But now I myself am also carried
810   beyond the laws when I see this.
I can no longer hold back the streams of tears,
when I see Antigone heading for
the bridal chamber where all must sleep.

ANTIGONE:[25]

                                                Str. 2

See me, O citizens of my ancestral land,

[23]*If Antigone starves to death, she will not technically have been murdered, according to Greek thought, and therefore there will be no pollution for her slayer. See* pollution *in glossary.*

[24]*the 3rd stasimon*

[25]*At this point, the stasimon becomes a kommos. See page 70.*

815 treading the final path,
gazing on the final light of the sun,
never again! But Death, the groom
of all, leads me alive
to the promontory of

26*a river in the Underworld*

820 Acheron;[26] I have no share
of marriage hymns, nor will any
hymn hymn me for my wedding
anyhow, but I shall be the bride of Death.

CHORUS:

Therefore, you will go famous and

825 honored into those depths of the dead.
Not stricken by wasting disease
nor taking the wages of the sword,
but, alone of mortals, you will go,
the ruler of yourself, down to Hades.

ANTIGONE:

Ant. 2

27*Niobe, a very famous mythological figure, punished for boasting about her children; see "Niobe" in glossary. Niobe is called the "Phrygian guest" because she was brought from Phrygia in Asian Minor to marry a Theban.*

830 I have heard that most sorrowfully did
our Phrygian guest die, the daughter of Tantalus, [27]
on the Sipylan cliff, how, like a vine of ivy,
the petrifying process overwhelmed her,
and the rain never leaves her,

835 languishing there, so men say,
nor does the snow ever leave her,
and beneath her tearful lids
she wets the ridges with her tears;
now my destiny sends me to a rest most like hers.

CHORUS:

28*The Chorus are not insulting Antigone, though she thinks they are. The Chorus merely remind Antigone that she is mortal, because it is always bad in Greek thought to compare yourself to a god.*

840 But she was a goddess and born of gods,
while we are mortals, of mortal race!
Still, it will be to your great fame,
as you die to share the lot of the god-like
while you live and, later, when you die.[28]

ANTIGONE:

Str. 3

845　Oh! I am mocked!
　　By our fathers' gods, why
　　do you outrage me, not yet departed,
　　but still in the light?
　　O city, O rich gentlemen of the city,
850　hail, springs of Dirce
　　and grove of many-charioted Thebes,
　　I'll yet have you as my witness,
　　how I have no friends to mourn me, by what laws
　　I go to the heaped-up prison
855　of my unheard of tomb.
　　Oh, my poor lot, who have no home
　　among mortals or corpses,
　　neither the living or the dead!

CHORUS:

　　You went forward far too boldly
860　and crashed into the lofty
　　pedestal of Justice, my child.
　　You are paying for your father's crime.

ANTIGONE:

Ant. 3

　　You have touched the most
　　painful of my cares,
865　the thrice-repeated doom of my father
　　and this whole fate of ours,
　　the famous Labdacids.
　　Oh, the sins of my mother's bed
　　and my ill-fated mother's
870　self-creating intercourse with my father!
　　From such as these I was born miserable!
　　I am going to live with them,
　　accursed, unwed.
　　Oh, my brother, you struck
875　an unlucky marriage,[29]
　　and dying you killed me, though I still lived.

[29] *a reference to Polynices' betrothal to the princess of Argos, because of which her father allowed Polynices to lead the Argive army against Thebes*

CHORUS:

> Reverence is a mark of character,
> but power, for a man who has it,
> does not tolerate offenses against itself.

880   Your self-guiding anger destroyed you.

ANTIGONE:

Epode

> Unwept, friendless, with no marriage hymn,
> unfortunate, I am taken
> down the prepared road.
> It is no longer right for unhappy me

885   to see this holy eye of light,[30]
> but no friend groans
> over my unwept fate.

[30]*the sun*

CREON:

> Don't you know that songs and lament before
> death would never stop, if they did any good?

890   Take her away at once, and shut her in
> her walled-up tomb, as I have said. Then leave
> her there alone, where she must either die
> or be entombed alive in such a house,
> for we have no guilt in this maiden's case...

895   Regardless, she'll lose her home in the world above.

ANTIGONE:

> O tomb, O bridal bower, o underground
> home everlasting, whither I journey
> to my own people, whose great number—
> so many destroyed—Persephone[31] has

[31]*wife of Hades and queen of the Underworld*

900   received among the dead. To these I go down—
> the last of them all and worst by far,
> before my allowance of life is spent.
> Nevertheless, as I go, I nurture
> the hope that I will come dear to my father,

905   dear to you, mother, and dear to you, my own
> dear brother. When you died, with my own hands
> I washed and adorned your bodies, and I poured
> libations at your tombs. But now, Polynices,

after burying your body, I reap
910 rewards like these. Still, I honored you well
in the eyes of the wise. No, if somehow
children whose mother I was or my husband
had died, I would not have undertaken
this labor in defiance of the citizens.
915 Shall I tell you the code I follow?
I could get another husband when mine died,
and a child from another man, if I
lost one from him, but since my mother and
father both lie in Hell, there is no field
920 where I could grow another brother.
With this as my law, I honor you above
all others; to Creon I seemed to have
made a mistake and to have done something
terrible, my brother. Now he holds me
925 thus in his hand and leads me, without a
wedding, no bridal hymn, I have no share
of marriage or raising children, but,
as I am, bereft of friends and unlucky,
I am going alive into depths of the dead.
930 Which of the gods' laws have I transgressed?
Why should I still look to the gods in my
unhappiness? What ally can I call?
In my case, by being pious, I have
won for myself the rewards of impiety.
935 But, if these men have sinned, may they not suffer
more evils than they unjustly inflict on me.

CHORUS:
The same violent winds
still rage in her soul.

CREON:
Therefore her guards will
940 suffer for their slowness.

ANTIGONE:
Alas, this word brings closer
my death.

CREON:

I'd be a liar to hearten you,
to say it's not certain.

ANTIGONE:

945 O ancestral town of Thebes
and primeval gods,
I am led away indeed,
no longer merely waiting.

CHORUS:[33]

Str. 1

Danae also dared to exchange
950 the light of day for walls of bronze;[34]
hidden away in a tomb-like
bedroom she was guarded.
Yet, her race was honorable,
O child, my child,
955 and she was the storehouse
of the golden-flowing seed of Zeus.
The power of fate is something terrible.
It cannot be escaped—not with wealth or by war,
not with a tower or a sea-lashed black ship.

Ant. 1

960 The son of Dryas,[35] quick to anger,
the king of Edonia, was yoked by stinging angers,
confined by the will of
Dionysus in a rocky prison.
Thus the flowering, terrible fury of his
965 frenzy dripped away. He learned
to know the god in stinging tongues,
whom he had provoked in his madness.
for he was stopping the races
of women and the Bacchic fire,[36]
970 he irritated the muses who love flutes.

Str. 2

Beside the sea's twin rocks, the Symplegades,[37]
the promontories of the Bosporus,
lies the Thracian Salmydessus,
where the city's neighbor Ares[38]

975 watched the accursed wound dealt
the two sons of Phineus
by his fierce wife,[39]
who blinded their avenging eyes,
smitten by her bloody hands
980 and the point of her needle.

Ant. 2

Wasting away unhappily, they mourned
their unhappy fate and their bastard
birth from their mother,
but her seed stretched back to the
985 ancient house of Erechtheus;[40]
in faraway caves,
her father nourished her in his hurricanes,
Boreas, swift as horses over the plains,
child of the gods. Yet against her, too,
990 the long-loved Fates pressed hard, my child.

Enter TIRESIAS *from offstage.*

TIRESIAS:
Lords of Thebes, with two watching from one,
we have come treading our common road,
for the road for the blind is from the guide.

CREON:
What news do you have, old Tiresias?

TIRESIAS:
995 I shall teach you, and you—trust the seer.

CREON:
It is not my custom to disagree with you.

TIRESIAS:
And thus you have captained this city correctly.

CREON:
I will testify that you have helped me.

[39]*Idaia, the second wife of King Phineus; see* Idaia *in glossary*

[40]*legendary first king of Athens*

TIRESIAS:
> Think now that you have walked onto a razor's edge.

CREON:
1000
> What is it? How I shudder at your words!

TIRESIAS:
> You will know when you hear the omens of
> my craft; for sitting on my ancient chair
> of bird-watching,[41] where in the past all the birds
> have gathered for me, I heard a strange new sound—
>
1005
> birds, screaming with evil, barbaric frenzy;
> and I knew that they were tearing at one
> another with bloody talons, for the rush
> of wings was clear. In fear, I went at once
> to test the burnt sacrifices on the
>
1010
> blazing altars, but no fire was burning
> on the victims. Rather, upon the embers,
> a dripping ooze trickled from the thigh pieces;[42]
> it smoked and sputtered, and the bile was scattered
> in the air, and the bones lay bare of the fat
>
1015
> that had covered them. Thus the omens failed,
> there were no signs, as I learned from this boy,
> for he is my guide, as I am to others.
> The city is sick because of your counsel,
> for our altars and all our hearths are defiled
>
1020
> by birds and dogs with carrion from the corpse
> of the unlucky son of Oedipus.
> For this reason the gods will not accept
> our sacrifices, prayers, and burnt thigh-bones,
> nor do the birds shriek forth clear-signaling cries,
>
1025
> gorged with a slain man's blood and fat. Therefore,
> think on these things, my child; for every
> human being makes mistakes, but when he has
> made a mistake, that man is no longer
> foolish and unhappy who remedies
>
1030
> the evil into which he has fallen
> and is not stubborn. Obstinacy brings
> the charge of stupidity. Yield to the dead,
> don't kick a fallen man! What prowess does

[41]*watching the sky for the movement of birds was an important part of Greek prophecy; see glossary*

[42]*see* sacrifice

it take to kill one already dead?
1035   My counsel is good, and so is my advice.
To learn from good advice is sweetest, if
the advisor speaks to your advantage.

CREON:
Go ahead, old man; all of you can shoot
your arrows at me like archers at targets.
1040   I am not even left untouched by the seers!
By your kind I was bought and sold and carried
home a long time ago. Make your profit,
purchase electrum[43] from Sardis, if you wish,
and gold from India; but you will not
1045   place him in a tomb, not even if Zeus's
own eagles[44] want to snatch up the carrion
and take it to the very throne of Heaven!
I will not allow him to be buried
out of fear of this pollution, for I
1050   know well that no human is strong enough
to pollute the gods.[45] But, the cleverest
of mortals, old Tiresias, fall with shameful
crash, when they decorate shameful words
for the sake of profit.

TIRESIAS:
1055   Foo.
Does any man know, does any consider…

CREON:
What thing? What great aphorism will you speak?

TIRESIAS:
…how much prudence is the greatest of possessions?

CREON:
(*sarcastically*)
As much as stupidity is the worst hurt?

TIRESIAS:
1060   You certainly seem full of this disease.

[43]*a valuable alloy of gold and silver, closely associated with the Lydian capital of Sardis*

[44]*the eagle was the bird of Zeus*

[45]*an idea contrary to traditional Greek piety, but in vogue with 5th-century Athenian human-ism and rational thinking.*

CREON:

    I don't want to return the seer's insult.

TIRESIAS:

    Yet you do when you say I prophesy lies.

CREON:

    The race of seers have always loved money.

TIRESIAS:

    And tyrants have always loved cheated profits.

CREON:

1065   Do you realize you speak these lies to your king?

TIRESIAS:

    I do, for your city is safe because of me.

CREON:

    You're a clever seer, but love injustice.

TIRESIAS:

    You will make me say the secret of my knowledge.

CREON:

    Do you think I say this for your profit?

TIRESIAS:

1070   Do I seem to do this as far as you're concerned?

CREON:

    Know that you'll not barter with my mind.

TIRESIAS:

    And you—know well that before the sun has
    run a few laps more, you will give one from
    your loins, a corpse for corpses, in exchange

1075   for those you have sent from above the earth
    to below it, the living soul you have lodged
    dishonorably in a tomb, and the

unhappy, unburied, unholy corpse
you hold back from the gods below. You have
1080 no share in this, nor do the gods below,
but this violence comes from you. For these things,
however, the destroying avengers
of Hell and the Furies[46] of the gods are
lying wait for you, that you may be taken
1085 in these same evils. Consider also
if I say these things as a hired accuser,
for a short time will reveal the wailing
of men and women in your house.
All the cities are stirred by hatred, whose
1090 mangled children took their only burial
from dogs and beasts—or some winged bird, bearing
an unholy stench into his native city.[47]
Since you hurt me, like an archer I have left
these words like unswerving arrows of the heart
1095 against your spirit, whose sting you will not escape.
Take me home, boy, so that this man may vent
his anger against younger men and learn
to keep his tongue quieter and fill his mind
with more elevated thoughts than he has now.

Exit TIRESIAS *and Attendant offstage.*

CHORUS:
1100 My lord, this man has gone after prophesying
terrible things, and we know that since I took
this white hair in place of black, he has
never spoken falsely to this city.

CREON:
I know, and I, too, am shaking in my heart,
1105 for to yield is a terrible thing, but it is
just as terrible to give up my anger.

CHORUS:
You must take good advice, child of Menoeceus.

CREON:
What should I do? Tell me, and I will obey.

[46]*ancient and terrible goddesses who avenged crimes committed against kin*

[47]*This indicates that all the Argive slain have been denied burial, not just Polynices.*

CHORUS:

>   Go and release the maiden from her rocky
> 1110   home and make a tomb for the unburied man.

CREON:

>   You advise this? You think I should yield?

CHORUS:

>   As soon as possible, my lord, for swift-footed
>   Divine Vengeance cuts down bad ideas.

CREON:

>   Alas, it is hard, but I give up what my heart
> 1115   wished to do. One should not fight necessity.

CHORUS:

>   Go now and do it, do not leave it to others.

CREON:

>   I'll go just as I am! Come, come, servants,
>   those here and those away—grab axes and
>   rush to that point over there. I myself,
> 1120   since my judgment has turned and seen better ways,
>   I bound her and I will go and release her,
>   for I fear that it is best to keep
>   the established laws as long as one lives.

CHORUS:[48]

Str. 1

>
>   Many-named one,[49] glory
> 1125   of the Cadmeian bride,[50]
>   offspring of loud-thundering
>   Zeus, you who protect famous
>   Italy, who are lord of
>   welcoming Eleusis[51]
> 1130   in the shelter of Demeter, O Bacchus,
>   inhabitant of Thebes, mother-city
>   of the Bacchants, by the flowing
>   stream of Ismenus, where the
>   dragon's teeth were sown.

[48]*Instead of a 5th stasimon, the poet has written here a hyporchema, or dance-song; the chorus is expecting a happy ending.*

[49]*Dionysus was also known as Bacchus, Iacchus, and Evius, to name just a few of his names. This ode, which anticipates that Creon will remedy the situation and save the day, is a hymn to Dionysus, It emphasizes the universality of his power and, accordingly, lists many places where he is worshipped.*

[50]*Semele, the Theban princess who was mother of Dionysus*

[51]*Dionysus, along with Demeter and Persephone, was worshipped in the Eleusinian mysteries; see glossary*

                                                    Ant. 1

1135   The flashing smoke
        has seen you
        over the double-crested
        rock, where Corycian nymphs
        go as your Bacchants
1140   by Castalia's stream.
        The ivy-covered slopes
        of Nysa's mountains and
        the green edge, rich in grapes, send you,
        visiting the streets of Thebes,
1145   while mortal tongues cry "Evoe!"[52]

                                                    Str. 2

        You honor this city
        above all others
        with your thunder-smitten mother,[53]
        but now, as the city and all her
1150   people are held by the violence of disease,
        come with cleansing fast over
        the cliff of Parnassus[54] or the lamenting crossing. [55]

                                                    Ant. 2

        Hail, dancing-master of the stars,
        breathing fire, overseer
1155   of the voices of the night,
        child of Zeus, appear,
        lord, together with your attendant
        Nymphs, who in their madness
        dance through the night with you, Iacchus, giver of gifts.

Enter the MESSENGER *from offstage.*

MESSENGER:
1160   Dwellers of the house of Cadmus and Amphion,[56]
        there is no sort of human existence
        I would ever praise or reproach as static.
        Chance sets us up and chance knocks us down,
            good luck
        and bad luck, always, and there is no seer
1165   who can tell a man what is destined for him.
        Creon was always enviable, I thought,

[52]*the ritual cry in honor of Dionysus, uttered by his ecstatic worshippers.*

[53]*Semele; see glossary*

[54]*the mountain at Delphi, which Dionysus shared with Apollo*

[55]*the strait between Boeotia, the region of Thebes, and the island of Euboea*

[56]*husband of Niobe who built the wall around Thebes*

who saved this land of Cadmus from her foes;
and after taking sole rule of the country,
he ruled, flourishing with a good crop of sons.
1170 And now he has lost it all, for when joy
betrays a man, I count him not as living,
but consider him an animated corpse.
Fill your home with riches, if you wish,
and live with a tyrant's bearing, but if you
1175 lose the joy of these things, I would not buy
them from a man for the shadow of smoke
in exchange for real pleasure.

CHORUS:
What new grief of our kings do you bring us?

MESSENGER:
They are dead, but the living are worthy of death.

CHORUS:
1180 And who slew them? Who has fallen? Tell us!

MESSENGER:
Haemon is lost. His blood was spilled by a
familiar hand.

CHORUS:
By his father's or his own hand?

MESSENGER:
Himself, angry with his father for the murder.

CHORUS:
1185 O seer, how correct your prophecy turned out!

MESSENGER:
With things like this, consider the rest besides.

Enter EURYDICE from the palace.

CHORUS:
>And now I see poor Eurydice here,
>Creon's wife. She comes from the house in
>mourning for her son, or perhaps by chance.

EURYDICE:
1190
>Citizens, I heard your words, as I was
>coming to the doors, so that I could go
>and pray before the goddess Athena.
>And just as I was opening the door,
>the sound of my family's misfortune
1195
>struck my ears, and I fell back, afraid,
>against my maids, and lost my senses.
>Still, tell the story again, whatever
>it is, for I am already used to trouble.

MESSENGER:
>Dear mistress, I shall say what I witnessed,
1200
>and I shall leave out not one word of the truth.
>Why should I soothe you with words that will later
>reveal me a liar? The truth is always right.
>I was following your husband as a guide
>into the farthest part of the plain, where
1205
>the unpitied corpse of Polynices,
>torn by dogs, still lay. There, asking the goddess
>of the crossroads[57] and Pluto[58] to hold back
>their righteous anger and bathing his body
>as custom demands, we gathered what was left
1210
>of him in newly-plucked branches, and, heaping
>a high tomb of his native soil, we headed
>to the stone-paved chamber of the bride of Death.
>Someone heard the shrill voice of mourning
>near the unhallowed chamber and pointed it
1215
>out to our master Creon. Who had uttered
>the tortured cry was still unknown to him
>creeping still closer, but he groaned and sadly
>said, "Am I the prophet of my own doom?
>Was it an unlucky road I traveled here?
1220
>The voice of my child greets me...servants, quick,
>go closer! Stand by the tomb and, at the gap

[57]Hecate, a witch-goddess associated with death and Artemis

[58]another name for the god of the underworld

in the rocks, find out if I recognize
the voice of Haemon or if the gods deceive me!"
At the command of our despairing master,
1225   we did observe; and in the last part of
the tomb, we saw her hanged by the neck, fastened
by a noose of fine linen, and him wrapped
around her, clinging to her around the waist,
bewailing the destruction of his lost bride
1230   and the deeds of his father and his unhappy
marriage bed. When the king saw them, he groaned
dreadfully and went inside towards the pair,
calling in lament, "Daring boy, what is
this thing you've done? What were you thinking?
1235   What misfortune has destroyed your mind?
Come out, child; as a suppliant, I beg you."
The boy glared at him wildly, spat in his face
and answered nothing, but drew his sword.
        He missed
his father, as he leapt away. Then, the poor boy,
1240   in his anger at himself, guided the sword,
leaned on it and thrust it into his ribs
up the hilt; and while he still had sense,
he pulled the maiden into his dying embrace.
With his dying breath he sent a river
1245   of crimson blood dripping down her white cheek.
There they lay, corpse on corpse, and, poor thing,
he got his wedding rites in the house of Death,
showing to humanity by how much
foolishness is the greatest evil for a man.

                        Exit EURYDICE *into the palace.*

CHORUS:
1250   What do you make of that? The lady has fled,
before she could say a word, good or bad.

MESSENGER:
I, too, am astonished, but I am fed
by hopes that she does not think it right to mourn
her son's fate in front of the city,
1255   but will set her maids to mourn their household's

grief under their own roof. She is not so
foolish that she would do something rash.

CHORUS:

I don't know: To me, excessive silence
seems to bode as ill as too much shouting.

MESSENGER:

1260   Then I will go and find out, lest she conceal
something hidden in her angry heart as
she goes inside the house. You are right:
There is also grief in too much silence.

Exit MESSENGER *into the palace.*

CHORUS:

And now the king himself approaches, bearing
1265   in his arms a memorial to,
if it is right to say it, no foreign
madness, but showing his own mistakes.

Enter CREON from offstage.

CREON:[59]

Str. 1

Oh!
Mistakes from thoughtless thoughts,
1270   stubborn and deadly!
O men who have seen
kin slaying and dying,
alas, for the misfortune of my plans!
Oh, my son—forever young by this untimely death,
1275   alas, alas!
You died, you were sent away
by my foolish counsels, not your own.

CHORUS:

I think you have seen justice too late.

CREON:

Alas!

[59]kommos

1280   I have learned pathetically,
         but then—oh, then some god was angry and hit
            me hard
         in the head and shook me on fierce roads,
         alas, overturned and trampled my happiness.
         Oh, the ill-labored labors of mortals!

Enter 2nd MESSENGER *from the palace.*

2nd MESSENGER:

1285   O master, you have enough evils already,
         the ones you carry now in your arms,
         and those in the house you will see soon.

CREON:

         What is left more evil than these evils?

2nd MESSENGER:

         Your wife is dead, the mother of this very corpse,
1290   poor creature, just now by recent strokes.

CREON:

Ant. 1

         Oh!
         Oh, haven of Death, so hard to appease,
         why, oh why do you ruin me?
         O you who have announced these
1295   grievous pronouncements to me, what word do
            you utter?
         Oh, oh! You have slain again a man already
            destroyed!
         What do you say, boy? Why do you tell me this news,
         alas, alas,
         this seal upon my ruin,
1300   to add on my wife's fate?

CHORUS:

         It is here to see, no longer hidden within.

60*See* ekkyklema

The body of EURYDICE *is rolled out upon the* ekkyklema. 60

CREON:

> Alas!
> Now I see this second, other evil.
> What, oh what lot still awaits me?
1305   I have just held my child in my arms,
> poor thing, and here is another corpse before me.
> Alas for the poor mother, alas for the child.

2nd MESSENGER:

> Stung by passion, at the altar she loosed
> her darkening eyes, lamenting first the
1310   famous death of Megareus, who died before,
> and then of this one, and last she called down
> evil fortune on you, the child-slayer.

CREON:

Str. 2

> Alas, alas!
> I am shaken with fear. Will no one strike
1315   me the mortal blow with a double-edged sword?
> I am a wretch, alas,
> and I am made whole by wretchedness.

2nd MESSENGER:

> Yes, and you are responsible for these deaths
> and hers whose corpse you see before you.

CREON:

1320   How did she come to die so bloodily?

2nd MESSENGER:

> She struck herself in the heart with her own hand,
> when she learned of the sad fate of her boy.

CREON:

> Woe is me, these things will never fall
> on another person so as to exonerate me,
1325   for I killed you, O unhappy
> I, I claim it truly. Servants,
> take me away right now, take me out of the way.
> I don't exist any more; I'm no one.

CHORUS:

    You offer good advice, if there is any good
1330   in suffering. The quickest solution
    is best when troubles are in your way.

CREON:

Ant. 2

    Go, go—
    let it appear, that most beautiful of all fates,
    the one bringing me my last day,
1335   the very best fate! Go, go—
    so that I may never look upon another day!

CHORUS:

    What will be will be. We must act on what lies
    before us. The future is the gods' concern.

CREON:

    That's all I was saying, my entire prayer.

CHORUS:

1340   Don't pray any more; it is not for mortals
    to escape our destined misfortune.

CREON:

    Let this rash man be led out of the way,
    who, my child, unwillingly slew you,
    and this woman, you, too—alas! I have
1345   no where to turn to, nothing to lean on,
    for everything goes cross in my hands,
    and a difficult fate falls on my head.

           Exit CREON, *led by Attendants, into the palace.*

CHORUS:

    Knowledge truly is by far the most important part
    of happiness, but one must neglect nothing
1350   that the gods demand.
    Great words of the over-proud
    balanced by great falls
    taught us knowledge in our old age.

Mythological Background

Since tragedies were based on widely-known myths or famous historical events, the audience would know the characters and outline of the story they were about to see. Most surprises, therefore, did not come from the plot, although playwrights could introduce innovations into the story. In seeing a play about Antigone, the audience would already know that this story came from the cycle of myths about the city of Thebes, one of Athens' rivals in the 5th century. The story is set a few generations before the Trojan War, which the ancients set in 1184 BCE. Laius, the king of Thebes, received a prophecy that his son would kill him. To avoid this outcome, when a child was born to Laius and his queen, Jocasta, he had the baby exposed on Mount Cithaeron, at the edge of his kingdom; he nailed the child's feet together as an extra precaution (a common way to get rid of unwanted infants throughout the historical period). Unfortunately for Laius, the baby survived and was raised as a prince of the city of Corinth with the name Oedipus, which means "swollen feet" in Greek.

Many years later, Oedipus, not knowing his true birth, met Laius on the road. Without either man knowing the identity of the other, an argument arose, and Oedipus unknowingly killed his father. At that point, Thebes was being terrorized by the Sphinx, a monster with the head of a woman, body of a lion, and wings of an eagle. The Sphinx was particularly famous for telling everyone she encountered a riddle; when they could not answer it, she devoured them. This was her riddle: "What walks on four legs in the morning, two legs in the afternoon, and three legs in the evening?" The person to solve this riddle was Oedipus, the answer being 'man' (who crawls as a baby, walks on two legs as an adult, but leans on a cane in his old age). Her riddle solved, the Sphinx threw herself from a cliff, and Oedipus was crowned king of Thebes and married to the recently widowed queen, his own mother Jocasta. Years passed before the gods brought the incest to light, after which Jocasta committed suicide and Oedipus blinded himself, living the rest of his life as a homeless wanderer.

Oedipus and Jocasta had several children together; when his sons disobeyed him, Oedipus cursed them, thus continuing the family's wretched destiny. Oedipus then died either at Thebes or in exile; the myths are inconsistent. Regardless, a quarrel arose between Oedipus' sons, Eteocles and Polynices. The latter, although older, was exiled and journeyed to the powerful city of Argos, where he won the favor of the Argive king. The king betrothed his daughter to Polynices, who returned to Thebes at the head of an Argive army. The panic-stricken city was defended by Eteocles and six others, who met Polynices and six heroes (the famous "Seven Against Thebes," subject of a play by Aeschylus) from the rest of Greece at each of the city's seven gates. The Thebans were victorious and the Argive army left the city. Polynices and Eteocles, however, were both slain, leaving the kingship to Jocasta's brother Creon. He also took custody of Oedipus' remaining children, two young daughters named Antigone and Ismene.

The Importance of Burial in Greek Religion

For the most part, the Greeks did not believe in a different afterlife for the good or bad—i.e., no heaven or hell. In their view, the afterlife was almost universally grim; the important detail for the dead was whether they were buried or unburied. Those who did not receive proper funeral rites were doomed to wander by the river Styx, the entrance to the Underworld, for eternity; their souls could never be at rest. Thus, denying burial to a corpse not only insulted the body, but also damned his soul for all time.

The buried were granted access to Hades, the name of both the Underworld and its king (who was also known as Pluto). In order for the dead to gain this access, a complicated ritual had to be performed. There were few 'professional' undertakers, so a man's funeral fell to his family, especially the women of the family. They prepared the body for cremation, oversaw the collection of the bones and ashes and burial of the urn, provided the tomb with liquid offerings (libations), and led the mourning, a loud and violent process in which women tore their cheeks with their fingernails, ripped out their hair, and poured dirt over the heads and clothing.

Mourning the dead was one of the few things women were allowed to do in ancient Greece, especially Athens. Women of well-born families were expected to stay at home in specially designated women's quarters at all times except during certain religions festivals. Marriages were arranged by a girl's father or guardian. Women were not true citizens of the democracy and could not speak or vote in the assembly. They were not even allowed to speak in court, a basic right for Athenian men.

Burying and mourning their dead relatives gave women an opportunity to do something important for their families. It brought women to the fore and gave them a role to play. When Creon forbids burial of Polynices, he denies Antigone the chance to do one of the few important things society allowed women to do. Thus, he is attacking her identity, and that is a large part of the reason she opposes his orders.

Greek Tragedy: An Overview

Tragedy and the City

Tragedy is particular product of the Athenian democracy. In the late 6th century BCE, the Athenians drove out the family of tyrants who had ruled the city for decades and established the only true democracy in western history. Almost all political offices were chosen by lot, and the assembly of all Athenian citizens voted directly on all important issues. It was during the 5th century that Athens became the most powerful city of Greece. After joining with other Greek cities to repel an invasion by the Persian Empire, the largest empire in the world at the time, Athens became an imperial power herself, conquering other Greek cities; eventually, though, the Athenians stretched their power too far and collapsed. Sparta and her allies conquered Athens in 404, and, although the democracy was restored and continued throughout the 4th century, Athens would never regain the glory she had achieved a century earlier.

5th-century Athens was almost unparalleled in its cultural achievement, from philosophy and science through architecture and the visual arts. Tragedy was the premiere literary genre of this period, and it is fitting that the apex of the democracy should be symbolized by a genre of poetry that involves the entire body politic. Performed at one of the major festivals of the city, the Great Dionysia, each tragedy was part of a contest. Three playwrights would be chosen by a city official, and each playwright would produce three tragedies and a satyr-play (a kind of farce intended to lighten the mood after three tragedies), all four plays being performed in a single day. The audience consisted of about 15,000 citizens, and the festival itself became a pageant of Athenian power and glory.

We know of many playwrights from this century, but the works of only three survived the end of antiquity and the Middle Ages, in which so much of ancient literature was lost. Fortunately, the three poets we have were universally considered to be the best: Aeschylus, Sophocles, and Euripides. From Sophocles, who won 20 victories (compared to Aeschylus' 13 and Euripides' four) we have the seven plays chosen by ancient critics as his finest: *Ajax, The Women of Trachis, Electra, Philoctetes,* and the so-called "Theban plays," *Oedipus Tyrannus, Oedipus at Colonus,* and *Antigone.* These three plays are not a trilogy *per se*; they were not written in order or performed together at one festival. In fact, about forty years separates the first play written, *Antigone,* from the last, *Oedipus at Colonus!* Each play, therefore, should be considered a separate work, and while Sophocles alludes to his earlier work, he pursued different goals and used different methods for each one.

The Genre of Greek Tragedy

Greek legend attributed to Thespis the invention of acting (hence we call actors "thespians"). Drama was born when, instead of just narrating events, an actor assumed a character and interacted accordingly with the chorus, who were also now seen as persons specific to the drama (hence, in the *Antigone*, the chorus is made up of the elders of Thebes). Both actor and chorus performed wearing elaborate costumes and masks. According to the philosopher Aristotle, Sophocles' predecessor Aeschylus added the second actor and Sophocles himself the third. With these three actors playing multiple roles (by changing their masks backstage!), a complete story could be acted out, and gradually the role of the chorus diminished. In the plays of Sophocles, the chorus rarely achieves the role of a real character as it so often does, for instance, in the plays of Aeschylus.

The plays followed a fairly strict structure, with a prologue, the entrance of the chorus, and then several episodes separated by choral odes. The dialogue of the plays is written in meter, but was spoken, like the plays of Shakespeare, whereas the choral odes were written in a more complicated meter to which the chorus could sing and dance. The plays also include a *kommos*, in which the main character(s) lament in song with the chorus. All in all, the form of Greek tragedy occupies a place somewhere between Shakespeare and opera. It is important, all the same, for modern readers to remember that they are getting a small portion of what the original audience received, for they are reading a *libretto* without the benefit of any music or the often elaborate costumes and scenery.

Conventions of the Genre

The most important convention of the Greek stage was the wearing of masks with attached wigs by all performers. As such, facial expression, which plays so large a role in modern theater, was not a factor. Additionally, the elaborate costumes worn by the actors and chorus members were often the most striking visual element. Staging was usually limited to the painted background behind the stage. Greek tragedies are all set outside, so this background usually depicted the exterior of the main characters' residence—in the *Antigone*'s case, the palace of Thebes. Changes of scene are rare in Greek tragedy, and props are kept to a minimum. The action of the drama takes place over a single day. In addition to the chorus and the three actors, mute characters could also appear on stage as needed. In front of the stage proper, which was not raised from the ground as in modern theaters, was a circular area called the *orchestra*, in which the chorus performed its dances. These would have musical accompaniment provided by an *aulos,* a double pipe like a modern oboe.

The Chorus

Since Greek tragedy grew out of the performances of lyric poetry sung by large choruses, it is only natural that the chorus should remain a large part of Greek tragedy. Every play's chorus (usually fourteen men) took on an identity appropriate to the play. For example, in the *Antigone*, they are old men of Thebes; in Aeschylus' *Eumenides*, they are the dread goddesses, the Furies.

The word chorus in Greek means "dance," and the chorus' main function was to sing and dance lyric *odes* in between dramatic episodes. These odes comment on the action of the preceding episode. An ode (also called a *stasimon*) usually consists of alternating stanzas, the *strophe* and *antistrophe*, which are in the same meter. Since odes are composed in lyric meters (as opposed to chanted iambic trimeters of the dialogue), these stanzas would be very complicated. Additionally, the main character(s) of a play could join the chorus in a *kommos*, a lyric song sung by both character and chorus at a point of heightened emotion.

The chorus was never on stage at the beginning of a play. Instead, after the play's prologue, the chorus members marched into the *orchestra*, the circular area beneath the stage where they danced. As they marched in, the chorus chanted a *parodos* to introduce themselves. The parodos is neither a lyric song or ordinary dialogue, but is metrically between these modes.

The chorus could also act as a character; one chorus member would be designated leader and speak lines of dialogue, interacting with the other characters on stage. They react as their characters should—in the *Antigone*, the Chorus are concerned with both religious and civic obligations; thus, they can see the good and bad sides to both Antigone's and Creon's arguments. They feel pity for both Antigone and Creon when they suffer, but they are not emotionally involved in the play's outcome the way the individual characters are.

Glossary

Argos – an important city in the Peloponnese (southern part) of Greece; in the 6th century BCE, Argos was one of the greatest cities in Greece. It is often considered the home of the legendary king Agamemnon, who led the Greeks in the Trojan War. By the 5th century BCE, when this play was written, Argos had faded from its leading position. It was still valuable to the Athenians, though, because it was a rival of their principal enemy, Sparta.

Birds – The Greeks thought that the gods communicated to mortals through birds. Different birds indicated different things, as did the actions of those birds. Since Tiresias is blind, he listens to the birds' cries for oracles, but Tiresias is an especially powerful seer and could prophesy just as well without birds.

Danae – a mortal woman beloved of Zeus; her father locked her in a room, which Zeus entered by assuming the form of a golden shower. The result of their union was the hero Perseus.

Ekkyklema – one of Athenian theatre's two 'special effects;' the ekkyklema was a wheeled platform which could roll out from behind the *scaena* (stage front), that is, from inside the house that served as backdrop of the play. It was usually used to roll out dead bodies of characters who had died in the house (since violence was almost never shown onstage). For instance, in Aeschylus' *Agamemnon*, Clytemnestra, having murdered her husband Agamemnon in the bath, declares her rule of the city of Argos while the ekkyklema rolls out to reveal the bloody corpse of the dead king.

Eleusinian mysteries – one of the most important cults in Greece; Dionysus, along with Demeter and Persephone, was worshipped in these mysteries. Unlike normal Greek religion, the cult promised salvation and paradise after death to believers.

Gods and goddesses – Greek religion was *polytheistic*; the Greeks worshipped many gods. The most powerful god was Zeus, the sky god, who was thought to have taken power when he overthrew his father, Cronus. After Zeus came the other Olympian deities, including Zeus' queen, Hera, his brother, Poseidon, and his children, Athena, Ares, Artemis, and Apollo. There were also other gods, older deities from the reign of Cronus who remained powerful and were considered irrational. Among these were the Furies, dread goddesses who hunted down and drove insane those people who killed blood-relatives.

The most important god for the *Antigone* is Zeus, who guards justice from his position as king of heaven. It was thought that Zeus protected Themis, a goddess who was a personification of 'right,' as opposed to 'wrong.' Themis enforced both the keeping of oaths and of humans' obligations to each other. Such enforcement ensured the orderly functioning of the universe and was therefore was very important to Zeus.

Justice – For the Greeks, justice meant doing good to your friends and harm to your enemies. The *Antigone* highlights the complications that could arise from this simple definition. Creon defines an enemy as anyone who turns against his city, but Antigone sees only family ties as sacred. Hence, they have different views of the fallen Polynices. Each, however, is convinced that his or her own course is just.

Idaia – the second wife of King Phineus of Thrace; she wanted to secure the kingdom for her own sons, so she blinded the sons of Phineus by his first wife, Cleopatra, who was the daughter of Boreas, the West Wind, and an Athenian princess. It is Cleopatra who is the analogy to Antigone, as Danae was.

Lycurgus – a Thracian king who denied the godhood of Dionysus as that god made his triumphal entry into Greece from the East. Dionysus responded by driving Lycurgus mad: After Lycurgus committed many crimes, he was arrested by his people and shut up in a cave, where he was killed by wild animals.

Maenads – throngs of ecstatic women who accompanied Dionysus; also called Bacchants. Their behavior was considered undesirable by ruling powers in various cities (Rome, for instance), who suppressed the cult of Dionysus.

Niobe – a queen of Thebes who had 14 children—seven sons and seven daughters; she boasted that she had more children than Leto, a goddess, who only had two. Unfortunately for Niobe, these two children were the powerful deities Apollo and Artemis, both of whom were associated with archery. Using their infallible arrows, Apollo and Artemis slew all of Niobe's children (Apollo killing the boys, Artemis the girls), and Niobe herself fled to a mountain, where she turned to stone, although never ceasing to weep (this phenomenon explained the image of a weeping woman formed by a spring in the porous limestone of the mountain).

Niobe is frequently alluded to in Greek literature because she is the perfect symbol for the suffering that comes, justly or not, from opposing or slighting authority. She was also the subject of tragedies in her own right, the most famous being that of the great playwright Aeschylus, whose play showed Niobe sitting on the stage, silently weeping, for over half of the drama before she said her first line.

Pollution – The Greek word is *miasma*, which means the pollution that comes from a crime offensive to the gods. Most often associated with a crime like murder or incest that violates natural law as well as human law, the idea could also be extended to cover not burying someone, which has obvious health risks in addition to religious ones.

Pollution affected both the agent and location of the crime, as well as any person or place harboring the criminal. Proper ritual cleansing (*katharsis*) was necessary to restore both person and place to an acceptable state. Antigone sees her brother's unburied corpse as miasma, and so she will do whatever is necessary to perform the proper rituals to end the pollution that keeps her brother from peace in the underworld. Creon, on the other hand, makes the rather revolutionary statement that men cannot pollute the gods, indicating his more modern 'humanistic' beliefs. Both views could be justified in 5th-century Athenian thought.

Prophecy – In order to understand the will of the gods, the Greeks used many methods of prophecy, which included consulting oracles (holy places in which humans could pose questions and receive answers through the god's chosen interpreter), inspecting the entrails of a sacrificed animal, or watching the motion of birds in the sky. All of this had to be done by a prophet, a specially chosen priest who could interpret such things. Tiresias is probably the most famous prophet in Greek myth, and the Athenian audience would know that whatever he said was true.

Sacrifice – Greek religion, for the most part, did not follow a moral code, but consisted of acts and prayers designed to win the favor of the gods. The ritual slaughter of an animal was considered the best way to do this, although other offerings could also be made, such as pouring a libation (liquid offering) of milk, wine, or honey or placing a gift of flowers or incense beside a statue of a god. Animal sacrifice involved slitting the animal's throat and collecting the blood in a bowl. The animal would then be slaughtered; the meat would be roasted and eaten by the humans performing the festival (generally the only time Greeks ate roasted meat), while the thighbones would be wrapped in fat and burned on the altar as a gift to the god. The priest would also inspect the entrails of the animal during the slaughter—if anything was amiss (for example, the liver was diseased or missing), it was a sign that the gods had not accepted the sacrifice and something bad was at work.

Semele – Another mortal woman beloved of Zeus; mother of Dionysus. Zeus's jealous wife Hera tricked Semele into asking Zeus to see him in his full glory as a god, which overwhelmed her mortal eyes. She burned to death, but Zeus grabbed the unborn Dionysus as she went up in flames.

Thebes – a city of Boeotia, in the northern part of mainland Greece. Thebes was one of the most famous ancient cities in archaic times, and many myths are set there. In the 5th century BCE, Thebes was a rival to Athens.

Vocabulary

aphorism – a proverb, saying
blithe – lighthearted, casual
concubine – a mistress
contentious – argumentative
edict – a decree
fratricidal – the killing of a brother
girt – surrounded
insolent – bold, impudent, contemptuous
lamentation – crying, wailing
languishing – wasting away
libations – liquids used in sacrifices to the gods
obstinacy – stubbornness
precepts – orders, rules
promontories – peaks, highest points
reproaches – disapproving comments
sires – to father
suppliant – a person making a request

Insightful and Reader-Friendly, Yet Affordable

Prestwick House Literary Touchstone Editions–
The Editions By Which All Others May Be Judged

Every Prestwick House Literary Touchstone Classic is enhanced with Reading Pointers for Sharper Insight to improve comprehension and provide insights that will help students recognize key themes, symbols, and plot complexities. In addition, each title includes a Glossary of the more difficult words and concepts.

For the Shakespeare titles, along with the Reading Pointers and Glossary, we include margin notes and eleven strategies to understanding the language of Shakespeare.

Special Introductory Educator's Discount – At Least 50% Off

New titles are constantly being added; call or visit our website for current listing.

		Retail Price	Intro. Discount
200102	Red Badge of Courage, The	$3.99	$1.99
200163	Romeo and Juliet	$3.99	$1.99
200074	Heart of Darkness	$3.99	$1.99
200079	Narrative of the Life of Frederick Douglass	$3.99	$1.99
200125	Macbeth	$3.99	$1.99
200053	Adventures of Huckleberry Finn, The	$4.99	$2.49
200081	Midsummer Night's Dream, A	$3.99	$1.99
200179	Christmas Carol, A	$3.99	$1.99
200150	Call of the Wild, The	$3.99	$1.99
200190	Dr. Jekyll and Mr. Hyde	$3.99	$1.99
200141	Awakening, The	$3.99	$1.99
200147	Importance of Being Earnest, The	$3.99	$1.99
200166	Ethan Frome	$3.99	$1.99
200146	Julius Caesar	$3.99	$1.99
200095	Othello	$3.99	$1.99
200091	Hamlet	$3.99	$1.99
200231	Taming of the Shrew, The	$3.99	$1.99
200133	Metamorphosis, The	$3.99	$1.99

PRESTWICK HOUSE, INC.
"Everything for the English Classroom!"

Prestwick House, Inc. • P.O. Box 658, Clayton, DE 19938
Phone (800) 932-4593 • Fax (888) 718-9333 • www.prestwickhouse.com